The
Messianic
Passover
Haggadah

"I have remembered my covenant." Exodus 6:5

Messianic Jewish Publishers
Clarksville, MD

Key for Pronunciation
of Hebrew Transliteration

An effort has been made to conform to
modern Israeli pronunciation of Hebrew.
We have adhered to the pronunciation key
below, except in cases where convention
has rendered a standard spelling.

- *"u" is pronounced "oo" as in "soon"*
- *"i" is pronounced "ee" as in "see"*
- *"a" is pronounced "ah" as in "hurrah"*
- *"ai" is pronounced "uy" as in "buy"*
- *"ey" is pronounced "ay" as in "day"*
- *"kh" and "ch" have no actual English equivalent;
  they are guttural sounds, which are
  made in the back of the throat*

Authors' note
This *haggadah* follows the format of a traditional *haggadah* with a
few exceptions made for ease of use and clearer understanding.

2022   13

2nd Edition
ISBN-13: 978-1-880226-29-2
Library of Congress Control Number: 2005921648

Published by Messianic Jewish Publishers
6120 Day Long Lane
Clarksville, MD 21029

Distributed by Messianic Jewish Resources International
For more Messianic Bibles and books, please visit our website.
Order line (800) 410-7367
E-mail lederer@messianicjewish.net   Website www.messianicjewish.net

 # reparing for Passover

For seven days you are to eat matzah [unleavened bread] — on the first day remove the leaven from your houses . . . Exodus 12:15

Leader

During the days before Passover, leavened items are removed from the home to make it ready. These include all breads and cakes, anything that contains yeast. Preparation begins with a thorough cleaning, culminating in a ceremonial search for leaven, called *bedikat khameytz.*

Let us also ready our hearts for the Passover *seder,* the order of service. Tradition teaches that in each generation, we must consider ourselves as having personally been freed from Egypt. As we prepare for this experience of personal redemption, let us put far from us the leaven of sin hidden within our hearts.

Haggadah means "the telling." Passover is a story that has been retold for thousands of years. It is a story of miraculous transitions — from slavery to freedom, from despair to hope, from darkness to light. Its greatness is the greatness of God. Its timelessness comes from the eternal truth of his involvement with his people. As God cared for the children of Israel in ancient times, he cares for all who are his today.

Upon the table is a *seder* plate, holding the ceremonial items of Passover. There are bitter herbs, a roasted egg, a sweet apple mixture, parsley, and a bone. Curious things, yet all part of the telling. Let us allow our senses to fully participate, taking in the sights and smells, tasting each ingredient, listening to every word. Let us see, hear, and feel the truth of God's love.

One of Messiah's last earthly acts was the celebration of the Passover. Gathering his friends in a small room in Jerusalem, he led them in a *seder*. "I have really wanted so much to celebrate this *Seder* with you" (Luke 22:15). He passed the foods among them. It was there, in celebration of the deliverance from Egyptian bondage, that Yeshua revealed to them the mystery of God's plan of redemption. He spoke to them of his body and blood. He explained to them that he would have to die.

It was no coincidence that Messiah chose the Passover for the setting of what is called by some, *communion,* or *the Lord's supper.* For in the story of the Passover lamb, Yeshua could best communicate the course he would be taking over the confusing hours that were to follow. Here, as we participate together in the Passover *seder,* may we recall once again God's great redemption.

בֵּיצָה
Roasted Egg

מָרוֹר
Bitter Herb

כַּרְפַּס
Parsley

Cup of Salt Water

חֲזֶרֶת
Horseradish Root

זְרוֹעַ
Lamb Shankbone

חֲרֹסֶת
Chopped Apples & Nuts

The Seder Plate

We Light the Candles

ADONAI is my light and salvation;
whom do I need to fear? Psalm 27:1

Leader

As we kindle the festival lights, we pray for the illumination of
the Spirit of God to bring great personal meaning to this, our
Messianic Passover celebration.

A Woman

(*Lighting the candles, says*)

בָּרוּךְ אַתָּה יְיָ אֱלֹהֵינוּ מֶלֶךְ הָעוֹלָם אֲשֶׁר קִדְּשָׁנוּ
בִּדְבָרוֹ וּבִשְׁמוֹ אֲנַחְנוּ מַדְלִיקִים הַנֵּרוֹת שֶׁל יוֹם טוֹב.

Barukh atah adonai eloheynu melekh ha'olam asher kidshanu bidevaro
uvishmo anakhnu madlikim haneyrot shel yom tov.

Blessed are you, O Lord our God, ruler of the universe, who
has set us apart by his Word, and in whose name we light the
festival lights.

Leader

As light for the festival of redemption is kindled by the hand
of a woman, we remember that our redeemer, the light of the
world, came into the world as the promised seed of a woman.
(Genesis 3:15)

 he Four Cups of Wine

ADONAI said to Moshe,
"Now you will see what I am going to do . . ."
Exodus 6:1

Leader

As the Lord spoke these words of encouragement to Moses, he revealed to his servant the plan by which he would redeem the children of Israel.

All

> ". . . I will free you from the forced labor
> of the Egyptians . . .
> rescue you from their oppression . . .
> redeem you with an outstretched arm . . .
> I will take you as my people, and I will
> be your God . . ." (Exodus 6:6, 7)

Leader

At Passover, we celebrate these promises of redemption by drinking from our cups four times. With each cup, let us remember the union that God desires.

The Cup of Sanctification

Kadeysh קַדֵּשׁ

". . . I will free you from the forced labor of the Egyptians . . ." Exodus 6:6

Leader

Let us lift our first cup together and bless the name of the Lord!

All

בָּרוּךְ אַתָּה יְיָ אֱלֹהֵינוּ מֶלֶךְ הָעוֹלָם בּוֹרֵא פְּרִי הַגָּפֶן.

Barukh atah adonai eloheynu melekh ha'olam borey pri hagafen.

Blessed are you, O Lord our God, ruler of the universe, who creates the fruit of the vine.

Leader

As he began his final Passover *seder,* Yeshua the Messiah shared a cup with his *talmidim* (disciples), and said to them,

> "Take this and share it among yourselves. For I tell you that from now on, I will not drink the ' fruit of the vine' until the Kingdom of God comes." (Luke 22:17, 18)

Let us all drink of this, the first cup of Passover.

We Wash our Hands
Urkhatz וּרְחַץ

Who may go up the mountian of ADONAI?
Who can stand in his holy place?
Those with clean hands and pure hearts . . .
Psalm 24:3, 4

Leader
(*Lifting the basin of water*)
Let us now offer the bowl of water to one another and share
in this hand-washing ceremony.
(*Pass the bowl of water along with a napkin or towel.*)

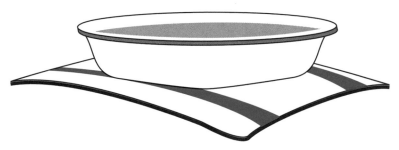

Let us also reflect upon the gesture of humility and the lesson
of commitment made by Messiah Yeshua, when, on that night,
he laid aside his garments and girded himself with a towel.

All

> Then he poured some water into a basin and began
> to wash the feet of the *talmidim* and wipe them off with
> the towel wrapped around him.
> He said to them, "Do you understand what I have done
> to you?" You call me 'Rabbi' and 'Lord,' and you are
> right, because I am.
> "Now if I, the Lord and Rabbi, have washed
> your feet, you also should wash each other's feet."
> (John 13:5, 12–14)

*P*arsley

Karpas בַּרְפַּס

. . . the people of Isra'el still groaned under the yoke of slavery, and they cried out, and their cry for rescue from slavery came up to God . . . Exodus 2:23

Leader

(*Lifting up the parsley*)
Passover is a holiday that comes in the springtime, when the earth is becoming green with life. This vegetable, called *karpas*, represents life, created and sustained by Almighty God.

(*Lifting up the salt water*)
But life in Egypt for the children of Israel was a life of pain, suffering, and tears, represented by this salt water. Let us take a sprig of parsley and dip it into the salt water, remembering that life is sometimes immersed in tears.

All

בָּרוּךְ אַתָּה יְיָ אֱלֹהֵינוּ מֶלֶךְ הָעוֹלָם בּוֹרֵא פְּרִי הָאֲדָמָה.

Barukh atah adonai eloheynu melekh ha'olam borey pri ha'adamah.

Blessed are you, O Lord our God, ruler of the universe, who creates the fruit of the earth.

Leader

Now let us, together, eat the *karpas*.

# The Four Questions

Ma Nishtanah   מַה־נִּשְׁתַּנָּה

*"When your children ask you,
'What do you mean by this ceremony?'
Say . . ." Exodus 12:26, 27*

A Young Child
(*Rising to ask the four questions*)

מַה־נִּשְׁתַּנָּה הַלַּיְלָה הַזֶּה מִכָּל־הַלֵּילוֹת!

שֶׁבְּכָל־הַלֵּילוֹת אָנוּ אוֹכְלִין חָמֵץ וּמַצָּה.
הַלַּיְלָה הַזֶּה כֻּלּוֹ מַצָּה.
שֶׁבְּכָל־הַלֵּילוֹת אָנוּ אוֹכְלִין שְׁאָר יְרָקוֹת.
הַלַּיְלָה הַזֶּה כֻּלּוֹ מָרוֹר.
שֶׁבְּכָל־הַלֵּילוֹת אֵין אָנוּ מַטְבִּילִין אֲפִילוּ פַּעַם אֶחָת.
הַלַּיְלָה הַזֶּה שְׁתֵּי פְעָמִים.
שֶׁבְּכָל־הַלֵּילוֹת אָנוּ אוֹכְלִין בֵּין יוֹשְׁבִין וּבֵין מְסֻבִּין.
הַלַּיְלָה הַזֶּה כֻּלָּנוּ מְסֻבִּין.

Ma nishtanah halailah hazeh mikol haleylot!

Shebekhol haleylot anu okhlin khameytz umatzah.
    Halailah hazeh kulo matzah.
Shebekhol haleylot anu okhlin she'ar yerakot.
    Halailah hazeh maror.
Shebekhol haleylot eyn anu matbilin afilu pa'am ekhat.
    Halailah hazeh shtey f'amim.
Shebekhol haleylot anu okhlin beyn yoshevin uveyn mesubin.
    Halailah hazeh kulanu mesubin.

How different this night is from all other nights!

On all other nights we eat bread or *matzah*.
　　On this night why do we eat only *matzah*?

On all other nights we eat all kinds of vegetables.
　　On this night why do we eat only bitter herbs?

On all other nights we do not dip our vegetables even once.
　　On this night why do we dip them twice?

On all other nights we eat our meals sitting or reclining.
　　On this night why do we eat only reclining?

We Answer the Four Questions

"You are to observe this as a law, you and your descendants forever."
Exodus 12:24

Leader
It is both a duty and a privilege
to answer the four questions of
Passover and to recite the mighty
works of our faithful God.

The Matzah
The Unleavened Bread

On all other nights we eat bread with leaven, but on Passover
we eat only *matzah*, unleavened bread. As the children of Israel
fled from Egypt, they did not have time for their dough to rise.
Instead, the hot desert sun baked it flat. But even more than
that, the scriptures teach us that leaven symbolizes sin.

All

> Don't you know the saying, "It takes only a little *hametz*
> [leaven} to leaven a whole batch of dough?" Get rid of the
> old *hametz*, so that youcan be a new batch of dough,
> because in reality you are unleavened. For our *Pesach*
> [Passover] lamb, the Messiah, has been sacrificed.
> (I Corinthians 5:6, 7)

During this season of Passover, let us break our old habits of sin
and selfishness and begin a fresh, new, and holy life.

Leader
(*Lifting the plate which contains the three matzot*)
This is the bread of affliction, the poor bread which our fathers
ate in the land of Egypt. Let all who are hungry come and eat.
Let all who are in need share in the hope of Passover.

Three *matzot* are wrapped together for Passover. There are
various explanations for this ceremony. The rabbis call these
three a "Unity." Some consider it a unity of the patriarchs —
Abraham, Isaac, and Jacob. Others explain it as a unity of
worship — the priests, the Levites, and the people of Israel.
We who know Messiah can see in this the unique *tri*-unity of
God — Father, Son, and Spirit. Three in one. In the *matzah* we
can see a picture of Messiah. See how it is striped.

All

But he was wounded because of our crimes,
crushed because of our sins;
the disciplining that makes us whole fell on him,
and by his bruises we are healed. (Isaiah 53:5)

Leader
See how the *matzah* is pierced.

All

"I will pour out on the house of David
and on those living in Yerushalayim;
a spirit of grace and prayer; and they will look to me,
whom they pierced." They will mourn for him as one
mourns for an only son . . . (Zechariah 12:10)

Leader
(Removing and breaking the middle *matzah* in half)
Just as the middle piece of the bread of affliction is broken,
Messiah, too, was afflicted and broken. One half is now called
the *afikomen* — "the coming one." It is wrapped in a white cloth just
as Messiah's body was wrapped for burial. (Wraps the *afikomen*)

If the children will cover their eyes, I will hide the *afikomen*.

Just as I have hidden the *afikomen*, so Messiah was placed in a tomb, hidden for a time. But just as the *afikomen* will return to complete our Passover *seder*, so the sinless Messiah rose from the dead to ascend into heaven. (*Break a piece of matzah from the other half of the middle piece and distribute the remainder among the people at the table.*)

Let us now share a piece of this unleavened bread of Passover.

All

בָּרוּךְ אַתָּה יְיָ אֱלֹהֵינוּ מֶלֶךְ הָעוֹלָם הַמּוֹצִיא לֶחֶם
מִן הָאָרֶץ.

Barukh atah adonai eloheynu melekh ha'olam hamotzi lekhem min ha'aretz.

Blessed are you, O Lord our God, ruler of the universe, who brings forth bread from the earth.

This is the bread of affliction . . .

The Maror
The Bitter Herbs

Leader

On all other nights we eat all kinds of vegetables, but on Passover we eat only *maror*, bitter herbs. As sweet as our lives are today, let us still remember how bitter life was for the children of Israel in the land of Egypt.

(*Lifting the horseradish*)
> . . . the Egyptians came to dread the people of Isra'el and worked them relentlessly, making their lives bitter with hard labor — digging clay, making bricks, all kinds of field work . . . (Exodus 1:12–14)

As we scoop some *maror* onto a piece of *matzah*, let us allow the bitter taste to cause us to shed tears of compassion for the sorrow that our ancestors knew thousands of years ago.

All

(*Lifting the matzah with the maror*)

בָּרוּךְ אַתָּה יְיָ אֱלֹהֵינוּ מֶלֶךְ הָעוֹלָם אַשֶׁר קִדְּשָׁנוּ
בִּדְבָרוֹ וְצִוָּנוּ עַל אֲכִילַת מָרוֹר.

Barukh atah adonai eloheynu melekh ha'olam asher kidshanu bidevaro vetzivanu al akhilat maror.

Blessed are you, O Lord our God, ruler of the universe, who has set us apart by his Word and commanded us to eat bitter herbs. (*All eat.*)

We Dip Twice
The Kharoset

Leader

On all other nights we do not dip our vegetables even once, but tonight we dip them twice. We have already dipped the parsley into the salt water.

(*Lifting the kharoset, the brown apple mixture*)
The children of Israel toiled to make treasure cities for Pharaoh, working in brick and clay. We remember this task in a mixture called *kharoset,* made from chopped apples, honey, nuts, and wine. Let us once again scoop some bitter herbs onto a small piece of *matzah.* But this time, before we eat, let us dip the herbs into the sweet *kharoset.*

All

(*Lifting the matzah with the maror and kharoset*)
We dip the bitter herbs into *kharoset* to remind ourselves that even the most bitter of circumstances can be sweetened by the hope we have in God.
(All eat)

Leader

As they were reclining and eating, Yeshua said,
"Yes! I tell you that one of you is going to betray me."
They became upset and began asking him, one after the other, "You don't mean me, do you?"
"It's one of the Twelve," he said to them,
"someone dipping *matzah* in the dish with me."
(Mark 14:18–20)

Tonight, We Recline

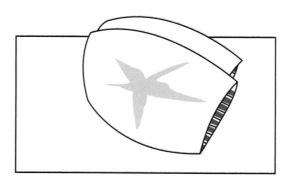

Leader

On all other nights we eat either sitting or reclining, but tonight we eat reclining.

The first Passover was celebrated by a people enslaved.

All

Once we were slaves, but now we are free!

Leader

The children of Israel were instructed to eat the Passover in haste, their loins girded, their staffs in their hands, their sandals upon their feet, awaiting departure from the bondage of Egypt. Today we all may recline and freely enjoy the Passover *seder*.

All

Messiah said,

> "Come unto me, all you who are struggling
> and burdened, and I will give you rest."
> (Matthew 11:28)

The Story of Passover

Magid מַגִּיד

"I have remembered my covenant."
Exodus 6:5

Leader

The story of Passover is a story of miracles, a story of redemption, a story of the mighty power of God to overcome evil.

Reader 1

The Lord had promised the land of Israel to Abraham, Isaac, and Jacob. Yet here were their children in Egypt. The Pharaoh who had come to power feared them. *These foreigners in our midst are prospering and have grown numerous,* he thought. *Suppose they join with our enemies and turn against us!* Pharaoh decided to exert greater control over this people, imposing harsh and bitter slavery upon the Israelites. Still, God blessed His people in strength and number.

Reader 2

Pharaoh grew more frightened and ordered every baby boy among the Israelites to be drowned in the Nile River. One Israelite couple hid their little boy for three months. Finally, entrusting his future to God, they set him in a basket and placed him upon the river. His sister, Miriam, watched as he floated downstream. Coming upon the basket, Pharaoh's daughter took pity on the child and chose to raise him as her own son. She called him Moses, meaning "drawn from the water."

Reader 3

Moses grew and became aware of the travail of his people. One day, in a rage, he lost control of himself and killed an Egyptian who was beating a Hebrew slave. Fleeing the palace and the eye of Pharaoh, Moses became a shepherd in the land of Midian, far from the cries of his suffering brothers.

Reader 4

The Lord, however, saw the affliction of the children of Israel and heard their groaning. He would raise up a deliverer to lead them out of bondage. It was then that He appeared to Moses in the midst of a bush that burned with fire, yet was not consumed. Moses drew close and listened as God commissioned him to go to Pharaoh. Fearful and reluctant, still Moses agreed to bring God's message to the king of Egypt, "Let My people go!"

I am the God of your father . . . the God of Avraham, the God of Yitz'chak and the God of Ya'akov.

Exodus 3:6

# The Cup of Plagues

"I will free you from the forced labor of the Egyptians . . ." Exodus 6:6

Leader

Moses left the wilderness to return to Pharaoh's palace, the very place where he had been raised. He returned with the message which the Lord had given him. But God Himself warned Moses of the resistance that he would encounter.

All

> "I know that the king of Egypt will not let you leave unless he is forced to do so. But I will reach out my hand and strike Egypt with all my wonders that I will do there. After that, he will let you go." (Exodus 3:19, 20)

Leader

God sent plagues, one by one, yet with each plague, Pharaoh hardened his heart. The Egyptians became afflicted with discomfort and disease, bane and blight. Still, Pharaoh would not relent. With the tenth and most awful plague, God pierced through the hardness of Pharaoh's impenetrable heart.

All

> "For that night, I will pass through the land of Egypt and kill all the firstborn in the land of Egypt, both men and animals; and I will execute judgment against all the gods of Egypt; I am *Adonai.*" (Exodus 12:12)

Leader

Let us fill our cups a second time. A full cup is a symbol of joy and indeed on this occasion we are filled with joy at God's mighty deliverance. But let us also remember the great cost at which redemption was purchased. Lives were sacrificed to bring about the release of God's people from the slavery of Egypt. But a far greater price purchased our redemption from slavery to sin — the death of Messiah.

As we recount each plague, let us dip a little finger into the cup, allowing a drop of liquid to fall, reducing the fullness of our cup of joy this night.

All

Blood!   Frogs!   Lice!   Beasts!

Cattle Disease!   Boils!

Hail!   Locusts!   Darkness!

Death of the Firstborn!

(*Do not drink the second cup at this time.*)

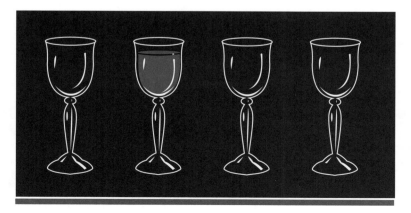

# he Passover Lamb

Pesach פֶּסַח

"The blood will serve you as a sign
 marking the houses where you are;
 when I see the blood, I will pass over you."
Exodus 12:13

Leader

Rabbi Gamaliel, teacher of Rabbi Saul (Paul, the Apostle),
taught that in recounting the Passover story one must be
certain to mention three things:

the Unleavened Bread	מַצָּה
the Bitter Herbs	מָרוֹר
the Passover Lamb	פֶּסַח

All

We have eaten the *matzah* to remind us of the haste with which
the children of Israel fled Egypt. We have tasted the bitter herbs
to remind us of the bitter slavery they experienced there.

Leader

(*Lifting the shankbone of the lamb*)
This roasted shankbone represents the lamb whose blood marked
the houses of the children of Israel, signifying their obedience to
God's command.

Reader 1

" . . . on the tenth day of this month, each man is to
take a lamb or kid for his family, one per household —

"Your animal must be without defect,
a male in its first year . . .

"You are to keep it until the fourteenth day of the month,
and then the entire assembly of the community of Isra'el
will slaughter it at dusk.

"They are to take some of the blood and smear it on
the two sides and top of the door-frame at the entrance
of the house in which they eat it." (Exodus 12:3, 5–7)

Reader 2

"That night, they are to eat the meat, roasted
in the fire; they are to eat it with *matzah* and *maror*.

"Here is how you are to eat it: with your belt fastened,
your shoes on your feet and your staff in your hand;
and you are to eat it hurriedly. It is Adonai's *Pesach*.

"The blood will serve you as a sign marking the houses
 where you are; when I see the blood,
I will pass over you — when I strike the land of Egypt,
the death blow will not strike you." (Exodus 12:8, 11, 13)

Leader

**We are reminded by Moses that it was the Lord himself who
redeemed the children of Israel from slavery.**

All

"And Adonai brought us out of Egypt with
a strong hand and a stretched-out arm,
with great terror, and with signs and wonders."
(Deuteronomy 26:8)

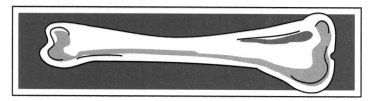

Leader
"For that night, I will pass through the land of Egypt . . .

All

I, and not an angel.

Leader
"and kill all the firstborn in the land of Egypt, both men and animals;

All

I, and not a seraph.

Leader
"and I will execute judgment against all the gods of Egypt;

All

I, and not a messenger.

Leader
"I am *ADONAI*." (Exodus 12:12)

All

I myself and none other.

Leader
Since the Temple in Jerusalem no longer stands, lamb is not eaten at Passover. This shankbone remains to remind us of the sacrificial lamb.

(*Lifting up the egg*)
Likewise, a roasted egg has been added to the *seder*. It is called *khagigah,* a name signifying the special holiday offering. The egg is regarded as a symbol of mourning, reminding us of the destruction of the second Temple. It is also considered by many to denote new birth and eternal life, since the shape of an egg shows no beginning and no end. The roasted egg may be eaten later, during the *seder* meal.

We who have trusted Yeshua the Messiah, believe *he* is the Lamb of God, our Passover. Like the ancient Israelites, we know that it was God himself, *and not an angel,* God himself, *and not a seraph,* God himself, *and not a messenger,* who achieved final redemption from sin and death. God himself, through Yeshua, who takes away the sin of the world.

So the Lord brought us out of Egypt

with an outstretched arm, with great terror and with miraculous signs and wonders.

# *Dayenu*

*It Would Have
Been Sufficient* דַּיֵּנוּ

*They will gush forth the fame of your abounding
goodness, and they will sing of your righteousness.
Psalm 145:7*

Leader

How great is God's goodness to us! For each of His acts of mercy
and kindness we declare *dayenu* — it would have been sufficient.

> If the Lord had merely rescued us,
>> but had not judged the Egyptians,   *All Dayenu!*
> If he had only destroyed their gods,
>> but had not parted the Red Sea,   *All Dayenu!*
> If he had only drowned our enemies,
>> but had not fed us with manna,   *All Dayenu!*
> If he had only led us through the desert,
>> but had not given us the Sabbath,   *All Dayenu!*
> If he had only given us the *Torah*,
>> but not the land of Israel,   *All Dayenu!*

But the Holy One, blessed be he, provided all of these blessings
for our ancestors. And not only these, but so many more.

All

Blessed are you, O God, for you have, in mercy, supplied *all*
our needs. You have given us Messiah, forgiveness for sin, life
abundant and life everlasting. Hallelujah!
(*Drink the second cup and sing Dayenu*)

The Passover Supper

Shulkhan Oreykh   שֻׁלְחָן עוֹרֵךְ

"... *a day for you to remember and celebrate as a festival to* ADONAI ..." *Exodus 12:14*
(*Leader gives a blessing before the meal.*)

he Afikomen

Tzafun צָפוּן

... being cut off from the land of the living for the crimes of my people ...
Isaiah 53:8

(If the afikomen has been "stolen" by one of the children, it may be ransomed back by the head of the table.)

Leader

It is time for us to share the *afikomen*, the dessert, the final food eaten at Passover. It is divided up as the Passover lamb was from the time of the exodus until the destruction of the Temple. It is said that the taste of the *afikomen* should linger in our mouths.

Messiah broke *matzah* and gave thanks to the Lord.

All

בָּרוּךְ אַתָּה יְיָ אֱלֹהֵינוּ מֶלֶךְ הָעוֹלָם הַמּוֹצִיא לֶחֶם
מִן הָאָרֶץ.

Barukh atah adonai eloheynu melekh ha'olam hamotzi lekhem min ha'aretz.

Blessed are you, O Lord our God, ruler of the universe, who brings forth bread from the earth.

Leader

It was then that Messiah added the words,
> "This is my body, which is being given for you;
> do this in memory of me." (Luke 22:19)

Let us now eat the *matzah,* meditating on the broken body of the Lamb of God who takes away the sin of the world. Let us allow the taste to linger in our mouths.

The Cup of Redemption

"I will . . . redeem you with an outstretched arm . . ."
Exodus 6:6

Leader

Let us fill our cups for the third time this evening.
(Lifting the cup) This is the cup of redemption, symbolizing
the blood of the Passover lamb. It was the cup "after the meal,"
with which Messiah identified himself. (Luke 22:20)

All

"I will . . . redeem you with an outstretched arm . . ." (Exodus 6:6)

Leader

The prophet Isaiah reminds us,

All   ADONAI's arm is not too short to save . . . (Isaiah 59:1)

Leader It is our own righteousness that falls short. Though the
Lord searched, He could find no one to intercede.

All   Therefore his own arm brought him salvation,
and his own righteousness sustained him. (Isaiah 59:16)

Leader Yeshua the Messiah lifted the cup, saying,

All   "This cup is the New Covenant, ratified by my blood,
which is being poured out for you." (Luke 22:20)

Just as the blood of the lamb brought salvation in Egypt, so Messiah's atoning death can bring salvation to all who believe.

All

בָּרוּךְ אַתָּה יְיָ אֱלֹהֵינוּ מֶלֶךְ הָעוֹלָם בּוֹרֵא פְּרִי הַגָּפֶן.

Barukh atah adonai eloheynu melekh ha'olam borey pri hagafen.

Blessed are you, O Lord our God, ruler of the universe, who creates the fruit of the vine. Let us gratefully drink. (*All drink.*)

The Prophet Elijah
Eliyahu HaNavi　אֵלִיָּהוּ הַנָּבִיא

Leader
(*Lifting the extra cup from Elijah's place at the table*)
This cup is for Elijah the Prophet, *Eliyahu HaNavi*. At this time let one of the children open the door to welcome Elijah to our *seder*. (*A child opens the door.*)

All

"Look, I will send you Eliyahu the prophet before the coming of the great and terrible day of ADONAI." (Malachi 3:23)*

Leader
Elijah did not see death, but was swept up to heaven by a great whirlwind, in a chariot of fire. It has been our hope that Elijah would come at Passover, to announce the Messiah, Son of David. Before the birth of John the Baptizer, an angel of the Lord said,

All "And he will go out ahead of ADONAI, in the spirit and power of Eliyahu. . . to make ready for ADONAI a people prepared." (Luke 1:17)

Leader Later Yeshua spoke of John,

All "Indeed, if you are willing to accept it, he is Eliyahu, whose coming was predicted." (Matthew 11:14)

Leader It was this same John who saw Yeshua and declared,

All "Look! God's lamb! The one who is taking away the sin of the world!" (John 1:29)

(*All sing Eliyahu HaNavi.*)   *Malachi 4:5 in some Bible versions

The Cup of Praise

Hallel   הַלֵּל

*I will take you as my people,
and I will be your God . . .
Exodus 6:7*

Leader

Let us fill our cups for the fourth and last time and give thanks to God, our great redeemer.

Give thanks to ADONAI, for he is good,
    All   for his grace continues forever.
Give thanks to the God of gods.
    All   for his grace continues forever.
Give thanks to the Lord of lords,
    All   for his grace continues forever;
to him who alone has done great wonders,
    All   for his grace continues forever;
to him who skillfully made the heavens,
    All   for his grace continues forever;
to him who spread out the earth on the water,
    All   for his grace continues forever;
to him who made the great lights;
    All   for his grace continues forever;
the sun to rule the day,
    All   for his grace continues forever;
the moon and stars to rule the night,
    All   for his grace continues forever;
to him who struck down Egypt's firstborn,
    All   for his grace continues forever;
and brought Isra'el out from among them,
    All   for his grace continues forever;
with a mighty hand and outstretched arm,
    All   for his grace continues forever;

to him who split the Sea of Suf*
> *All for his grace continues forever;*

and made Isra'el cross right through it,
> *All for his grace continues forever;*

but swept Pharaoh and his army into the Sea of Suf,
> *All for his grace continues forever;*

to him who led his people through the desert,
> *All for his grace continues forever;*

Give thanks to the God of heaven.
> *All for his grace continues forever.*
> (Psalm 136:1–16, 26)

Leader

(*Lifting the cup*)
Let us lift our cups and bless the name of the Lord!

All

בָּרוּךְ אַתָּה יְיָ אֱלֹהֵינוּ מֶלֶךְ הָעוֹלָם בּוֹרֵא פְּרִי הַגָּפֶן.

Barukh atah adonai eloheynu melekh ha'olam borey pri hagafen.

Blessed are you, O Lord our God, ruler of the universe,
who creates the fruit of the vine.

Leader

Our Passover *seder* is now complete, just as our redemption in Messiah is forever complete. Let us conclude with the traditional wish that we may celebrate Passover next year in Jerusalem.

*Sea of Reeds

לַשָׁנָה הַבָּאָה בִּירוּשָׁלַיִם.

Lashanah haba'ah bi Yerushalayim.

Next year in Jerusalem!

(All sing Lashanah Haba'ah)

Dayenu
It Would Have Been Sufficient
דינו

If God had merely rescued us from Egypt, Dayenu, it would have been sufficient.

(Other verses:)

> Ilu notan notan lonu,
> Notan lonu et ha *Torah*,
> Notan lonu et ha *Torah*,
> *Dayenu!* (sing chorus)

If God had merely given us the Law (Scriptures), Dayenu, it would have been sufficient.

> Ilu notan notan lonu,
> Notan lonu et Yeshua
> Notan lonu et Yeshua,
> *Dayenu!* (sing chorus)

Since God has given us Yeshua (the Messiah), Dayenu, he is sufficient!

Lashanah Haba'ah bi Yerushalayim, *final measures,* *continued from page 36*

Eliyahu HaNavi
Elijah the Prophet
אליהו הנביא

May the prophet Elijah come soon, in our time, with the Messiah, son of David.

E - li - yo - hu ha - no - vi, E - li - yo - hu
ha - tish - bi, E - li - yo - hu, E - li - yo - hu, E - li - yo - hu ha -
gil - o - di. Bim' - hey - ro v' - yo - mey - nu. Yo - vo e - ley - nu.
Im Mo - shi - ah ben Do - vid, Im Mo - shi - ah ben Do - vid.

Lashanah Haba'ah bi Yerushalayim
Next Year in Jerusalem
לשנה הבאה בירושלים

 Continued on page 34